Mental Efficiency. And Other Hints to Men and Women

by

Arnold Bennett

The Echo Library 2008

Published by

The Echo Library

Echo Library
131 High St.
Teddington
Middlesex TW11 8HH

www.echo-library.com

ISBN 978-1-40686-673-5

CONTENTS

I

MENTAL EFFICIENCY

THE APPEAL

If there is any virtue in advertisements—and a journalist should be the last person to say that there is not—the American nation is rapidly reaching a state of physical efficiency of which the world has probably not seen the like since Sparta. In all the American newspapers and all the American monthlies are innumerable illustrated announcements of "physical-culture specialists," who guarantee to make all the organs of the body perform their duties with the mighty precision of a 60 h.p. motor-car that never breaks down. I saw a book the other day written by one of these specialists, to show how perfect health could be attained by devoting a quarter of an hour a day to certain exercises. The advertisements multiply and increase in size. They cost a great deal of money. Therefore they must bring in a great deal of business. Therefore vast numbers of people must be worried about the non-efficiency of their bodies, and on the way to achieve efficiency. In our more modest British fashion, we have the same phenomenon in England. And it is growing. Our muscles are growing also. Surprise a man in his bedroom of a morning, and you will find him lying on his back on the floor, or standing on his head, or whirling clubs, in pursuit of physical efficiency. I remember that once I "went in" for physical efficiency myself. I, too, lay on the floor, my delicate epidermis separated from the carpet by only the thinnest of garments, and I contorted myself according to the fifteen diagrams of a large chart (believed to be the *magna charta* of physical efficiency) daily after shaving. In three weeks my collars would not meet round my prize-fighter's neck; my hosier reaped immense profits, and I came to the conclusion that I had carried physical efficiency quite far enough.

A strange thing—was it not?—that I never had the idea of devoting a quarter of an hour a day after shaving to the pursuit of mental efficiency. The average body is a pretty complicated affair, sadly out of order, but happily susceptible to culture. The average mind is vastly more complicated, not less sadly out of order, but perhaps even more susceptible to culture. We compare our arms to the arms of the gentleman illustrated in the physical efficiency advertisement, and we murmur to ourselves the classic phrase: "This will never do." And we set about developing the muscles of our arms until we can show them off (through a frock coat) to women at afternoon tea. But it does not, perhaps, occur to us that the mind has its muscles, and a lot of apparatus besides, and that these invisible, yet paramount, mental organs are far less efficient than they ought to be; that some of them are atrophied, others starved, others out of shape, etc. A man of sedentary occupation goes for a very long walk on Easter Monday, and in the evening is so exhausted that he can scarcely eat. He wakes up to the inefficiency of his body, caused by his neglect of it, and he is so shocked that he determines on remedial measures. Either he will walk to the office, or he will play golf, or he will execute the post-shaving exercises. But let the same man after a prolonged sedentary course of newspapers, magazines, and novels, take his mind out for a stiff climb among the rocks of a scientific, philosophic, or artistic subject. What will he do? Will he stay out all day, and return in the evening too tired even to read his paper? Not he. It is ten to one that, finding himself puffing for breath after a quarter of an hour, he won't even persist till he gets his second wind, but will come back at once. Will he remark with genuine concern that his mind is sadly out of condition and that he really must do something to get it into order? Not he. It is a hundred to one that he will tranquilly accept the *status quo*, without shame and without very poignant regret. Do I make my meaning clear?

I say, without a *very poignant* regret, because a certain vague regret is indubitably caused by realizing that one is handicapped by a mental inefficiency which might, without too much difficulty, be cured. That vague regret exudes like a vapour from the more cultivated section of the public. It is to be detected everywhere, and especially among people who are near the half-way house of life. They perceive the existence of immense quantities of knowledge, not the smallest particle of which will they ever make their own. They stroll forth from their orderly dwellings on a starlit night, and feel dimly the wonder of the heavens. But the still small voice is telling them that, though they have read in a newspaper that there are fifty thousand stars in the Pleiades, they cannot even point to the Pleiades in the sky. How they would like to grasp the significance of the nebular theory, the most overwhelming of all theories! And the years are passing; and there are twenty-four hours in every day, out of which they work only six or seven; and it needs only an impulse, an effort, a system, in order gradually to cure the mind of its slackness, to give "tone" to its muscles, and to enable it to grapple with the splendours of knowledge and sensation that await it! But the regret is not poignant enough. They do nothing. They go on doing nothing. It is as though they passed for ever along the length of an endless table filled with delicacies, and could not stretch out a hand to seize. Do I exaggerate? Is there not deep in the consciousness of most of us a mournful feeling that our minds are like the liver of the advertisement—sluggish, and that for the sluggishness of our minds there is the excuse neither of incompetence, nor of lack of time, nor of lack of opportunity, nor of lack of means?

Why does not some mental efficiency specialist come forward and show us how to make our minds do the work which our minds are certainly capable of doing? I do not mean a quack. All the physical efficiency specialists who advertise largely are not quacks. Some of them achieve very genuine results. If a course of treatment can be devised for the body, a course of treatment can be devised for the mind. Thus we might realize some of the ambitions which all of us cherish in regard to the utilization in our spare time of that magnificent machine which we allow to rust within our craniums. We have the desire to perfect ourselves, to round off our careers with the graces of knowledge and taste. How many people would not gladly undertake some branch of serious study, so that they might not die under the reproach of having lived and died without ever really having known anything about anything! It is not the absence of desire that prevents them. It is, first, the absence of will-power—not the will to begin, but the will to continue; and, second, a mental apparatus which is out of condition, "puffy," "weedy," through sheer neglect. The remedy, then, divides itself into two parts, the cultivation of will-power, and the getting into condition of the mental apparatus. And these two branches of the cure must be worked concurrently.

I am sure that the considerations which I have presented to you must have already presented themselves to tens of thousands of my readers, and that thousands must have attempted the cure. I doubt not that many have succeeded. I shall deem it a favour if those readers who have interested themselves in the question will communicate to me at once the result of their experience, whatever its outcome. I will make such use as I can of the letters I receive, and afterwards I will give my own experience.

THE REPLIES

The correspondence which I have received in answer to my appeal shows that at any rate I did not overstate the case. There is, among a vast mass of reflecting people in this country, a clear consciousness of being mentally less than efficient, and a strong (though ineffective) desire that such mental inefficiency should cease to be. The desire is stronger than I had imagined, but it does not seem to have led to much hitherto. And that "course of treatment for the mind," by means of which we are to "realize some of the ambitions which all of us cherish in regard to the utilization in our spare time of the magnificent machine which we allow to rust within our craniums"—that desiderated course of treatment has not apparently been devised by anybody. The Sandow of the brain has not yet loomed up above the horizon. On the other hand, there appears to be a general expectancy that I personally am going to play the rôle of the Sandow of the brain. Vain thought!

I have been very much interested in the letters, some of which, as a statement of the matter in question, are admirable. It is perhaps not surprising that the best of them come from women—for (genius apart) woman is usually more touchingly lyrical than man in the yearning for the ideal. The most enthusiastic of all the letters I have received, however, is from a gentleman whose notion is that we should be hypnotised into mental efficiency. After advocating the establishment of "an institution of practical psychology from whence there can be graduated fit and proper people whose efforts would be in the direction of the subconscious mental mechanism of the child or even the adult," this hypnotist proceeds: "Between the academician, whose specialty is an inconsequential cobweb, the medical man who has got it into his head that he is the logical foster-father for psychonomical matters, and the blatant 'professor' who deals with monkey tricks on a few somnambules on the music-hall stage, you are allowing to go unrecognized one of the most potent factors of mental development." Am I? I have not the least idea what this gentleman means, but I can assure him that he is wrong. I can make more sense out of the remarks of another correspondent who, utterly despising the things of the mind, compares a certain class of young men to "a halfpenny bloater with the roe out," and asserts that he himself "got out of the groove" by dint of having to unload ten tons of coal in three hours and a half every day during several years. This is interesting and it is constructive, but it is just a little beside the point.

A lady, whose optimism is indicated by her pseudonym, "Espérance," puts her finger on the spot, or, rather, on one of the spots, in a very sensible letter. "It appears to me," she says, "that the great cause of mental inefficiency is lack of concentration, perhaps especially in the case of women. I can trace my chief failures to this cause. Concentration, is a talent. It may be in a measure cultivated, but it needs to be inborn.... The greater number of us are in a state of semi-slumber, with minds which are only exerted to one-half of their capability." I thoroughly agree that inability to concentrate is one of the chief symptoms of the mental machine being out of condition. "Espérance's" suggested cure is rather drastic. She says: "Perhaps one of the best cures for mental sedentariness is arithmetic, for there is nothing else which requires greater power of concentration." Perhaps arithmetic might be an effective cure, but it is not a practical cure, because no one, or scarcely any one, would practise it. I cannot imagine the plain man who, having a couple of hours to spare of a night, and having also the sincere desire but not the will-power to improve his taste and knowledge, would deliberately sit down and work sums by way of preliminary mental calisthenics. As Ibsen's puppet said: "People don't do these things." Why do they not? The answer is: Simply because they won't; simply because human nature will not run to it. "Espérance's" suggestion of learning poetry is slightly better.

Certainly the best letter I have had is from Miss H. D. She says: "This idea [to avoid the reproach of 'living and dying without ever really knowing anything about anything'] came to me of itself from somewhere when I was a small girl. And looking back I fancy that the thought itself spurred me to do something in this world, to get into line with people who did things—people who painted pictures, wrote books, built bridges, or did something beyond the ordinary. This only has seemed to me, all my life since, worth while." Here I must interject that such a statement is somewhat sweeping. In fact, it sweeps a whole lot of fine and legitimate ambitions straight into the rubbish heap of the Not-worth-while. I think the writer would wish to modify it. She continues: "And when the day comes in which I have not done some serious reading, however small the measure, or some writing ... or I have been too sad or dull to notice the brightness of colour of the sun, of grass and flowers, of the sea, or the moonlight on the water, I think the day ill-spent. So I must think the *incentive* to do a little each day beyond the ordinary towards the real culture of the mind, is the beginning of the cure of mental inefficiency." This is very ingenious and good. Further: "The day comes when the mental habit has become a part of our life, and we value mental work for the work's sake." But I am not sure about that. For myself, I have never valued work for its own sake, and I never shall. And I only value such mental work for the more full and more intense consciousness of being alive which it gives me.

Miss H. D.'s remedies are vague. As to lack of will-power, "the first step is to realize your weakness; the next step is to have ordinary shame that you are defective." I doubt, I gravely doubt, if these steps would lead to anything definite. Nor is this very helpful: "I would advise reading, observing, writing. I would advise the use of every sense and every faculty by which we at last learn the sacredness of life." This is begging the question. If people, by merely wishing to do so, could regularly and seriously read, observe, write, and use every faculty and sense, there would be very little mental inefficiency. I see that I shall be driven to construct a programme out of my own bitter and ridiculous experiences.

THE CURE

"But tasks in hours of insight willed
Can be through hours of gloom fulfilled."

The above lines from Matthew Arnold are quoted by one of my very numerous correspondents to support a certain optimism in this matter of a systematic attempt to improve the mind. They form part of a beautiful and inspiring poem, but I gravely fear that they run counter to the vast mass of earthly experience. More often than not I have found that a task willed in some hour of insight can *not* be fulfilled through hours of gloom. No, no, and no! To will is easy: it needs but the momentary bright contagion of a stronger spirit than one's own. To fulfil, morning after morning, or evening after evening, through months and years—this is the very dickens, and there is not one of my readers that will not agree with me. Yet such is the elastic quality of human nature that most of my correspondents are quite ready to ignore the sad fact and to demand at once: "what shall we will? Tell us what we must will." Some seem to think that they have solved the difficulty when they have advocated certain systems of memory and mind-training. Such systems may be in themselves useful or useless—the evidence furnished to me is contradictory—but were they perfect systems, a man cannot be intellectually born again merely by joining a memory-class. The best system depends utterly on the man's power of resolution. And what really counts is not the system, but the spirit in which the man handles it. Now, the proper spirit can only be induced by a careful consideration and realization of the man's conditions—the limitations of his temperament, the strength of adverse influences, and the lessons of his past.

Let me take an average case. Let me take your case, O man or woman of thirty, living in comfort, with some cares, and some responsibilities, and some pretty hard daily work, but not too much of any! The question of mental efficiency is in the air. It interests you. It touches you nearly. Your conscience tells you that your mind is less active and less informed than it might be. You suddenly spring up from the garden-seat, and you say to yourself that you will take your mind in hand and do something with it. Wait a moment. Be so good as to sink back into that garden-seat and clutch that tennis racket a little longer. You have had these "hours of insight" before, you know. You have not arrived at the age of thirty without having tried to carry out noble resolutions—and failed. What precautions are you going to take against failure this time? For your will is probably no stronger now than it was aforetime. You have admitted and accepted failure in the past. And no wound is more cruel to the spirit of resolve than that dealt by failure. You fancy the wound closed, but just at the critical moment it may reopen and mortally bleed you. What are your precautions? Have you thought of them? No. You have not.

I have not the pleasure of your acquaintance. But I know you because I know myself. Your failure in the past was due to one or more of three causes. And the first was that you undertook too much at the beginning. You started off with a magnificent programme. You are something of an expert in physical exercises—you would be ashamed not to be, in these physical days—and so you would never attempt a hurdle race or an uninterrupted hour's club-whirling without some preparation. The analogy between the body and the mind ought to have struck you. *This* time, please do not form an elaborate programme. Do not form any programme. Simply content yourself with a preliminary canter, a ridiculously easy preliminary canter. For example (and I give this merely as an example), you might say to yourself: "Within one month from this date I will read twice Herbert Spencer's little book on 'Education'—sixpence—and will make notes in pencil inside the back cover of the things that particularly strike me." You remark that that is nothing, that you can do it "on your head," and so on. Well, do it. When it is done you will at any rate possess the satisfaction of having resolved to do something and having done it. Your mind will have gained tone and healthy pride. You will be even justified in setting yourself some kind of a simple programme to extend over three months. And you will have acquired some general principles by the light of which to construct the programme. But best of all, you will have avoided failure, that dangerous wound.

The second possible cause of previous failure was the disintegrating effect on the will-power of the ironic, superior smile of friends. Whenever a man "turns over a new leaf" he has this inane giggle to face. The drunkard may be less ashamed of getting drunk than of breaking to a crony the news that he has signed the pledge. Strange, but true! And human nature must be counted with. Of course, on a few stern spirits the effect of that smile is merely to harden the resolution. But on the majority its influence is deleterious. Therefore don't go and nail your flag to the mast. Don't raise any flag. Say nothing. Work as unobtrusively as you can. When you have won a battle or two you can begin to wave the banner, and then you will find that that miserable, pitiful, ironic, superior smile will die away ere it is born.

The third possible cause was that you did not rearrange your day. Idler and time-waster though you have been, still you had done *something* during the twenty-four hours. You went to work with a kind of dim idea that there were twenty-six hours in every day. *Something large and definite has to be dropped.* Some space in the rank jungle of the day has to be cleared and swept up for the new operations. Robbing yourself of sleep won't help you, nor trying to "squeeze in" a time for study between two other times. Use the knife, and use it freely. If you mean to read or think half an hour a day, arrange for an hour. A hundred per cent. margin is not too much for a beginner. Do you ask me where the knife is to be used? I should say that in nine cases out of ten the rites of the cult of the body might be abbreviated. I recently spent a week-end in a London suburb, and I was staggered by the wholesale attention given to physical recreation in all its forms. It was a gigantic debauch of the muscles on every side. It shocked me. "Poor withering mind!" I thought. "Cricket, and football, and boating, and golf, and tennis have their 'seasons,' but not thou!" These considerations are general and prefatory. Now I must come to detail.

MENTAL CALISTHENICS

I have dealt with the state of mind in which one should begin a serious effort towards mental efficiency, and also with the probable causes of failure in previous efforts. We come now to what I may call the calisthenics of the business, exercises which may be roughly compared to the technical exercises necessary in learning to play a musical instrument. It is curious that a person studying a musical instrument will have no false shame whatever in doing mere exercises for the fingers and wrists while a person who is trying to get his mind into order will almost certainly experience a false shame in going through performances which are undoubtedly good for him. Herein lies one of the great obstacles to mental efficiency. Tell a man that he should join a memory class, and he will hum and haw, and say, as I have already remarked, that memory isn't everything; and, in short, he won't join the memory class, partly from indolence, I grant, but more from false shame. (Is not this true?) He will even hesitate about learning things by heart. Yet there are few mental exercises better than learning great poetry or prose by heart. Twenty lines a week for six months: what a "cure" for debility! The chief, but not the only, merit of learning by heart as an exercise is that it compels the mind to concentrate. And the most important preliminary to self-development is the faculty of concentrating at will. Another excellent exercise is to read a page of no-matter-what, and then immediately to write down—in one's own words or in the author's—one's full recollection of it. A quarter of an hour a day! No more! And it works like magic.

This brings me to the department of writing. I am a writer by profession; but I do not think I have any prejudices in favour of the exercise of writing. Indeed, I say to myself every morning that if there is one exercise in the world which I hate, it is the exercise of writing. But I must assert that in my opinion the exercise of writing is an indispensable part of any genuine effort towards mental efficiency. I don't care much what you write, so long as you compose sentences and achieve continuity. There are forty ways of writing in an unprofessional manner, and they are all good. You may keep "a full diary," as Mr. Arthur Christopher Benson says he does. This is one of the least good ways. Diaries, save in experienced hands like those of Mr. Benson, are apt to get themselves done with the very minimum of mental effort. They also tend to an exaggeration of egotism, and if they are left lying about they tend to strife. Further, one never knows when one may not be compelled to produce them in a court of law. A journal is better. Do not ask me to define the difference between a journal and a diary. I will not and I cannot. It is a difference that one feels instinctively. A diary treats exclusively of one's self and one's doings; a journal roams wider, and notes whatever one has observed of interest. A diary relates that one had lobster mayonnaise for dinner and rose the next morning with a headache, doubtless attributable to mental strain. A journal relates that Mrs. ——, whom one took into dinner, had brown eyes, and an agreeable trick of throwing back her head after asking a question, and gives her account of her husband's strange adventures in Colorado, etc. A diary is

All I, I, I, I, itself I

(to quote a line of the transcendental poetry of Mary Baker G. Eddy). A journal is the large spectacle of life. A journal may be special or general. I know a man who keeps a journal of all cases of current superstition which he actually encounters. He began it without the slightest suspicion that he was beginning a document of astounding interest and real scientific value; but such was the fact. In default of a diary or a journal, one may write essays (provided one has the moral courage); or one may simply make notes on the book one reads. Or one may construct anthologies of passages which have made an individual and particular appeal to one's tastes. Anthology construction is one of the pleasantest hobbies that a person who is not mad about golf and bridge—that is to say, a thinking person—can possibly have; and I recommend it to those who, discreetly mistrusting their power to keep up a fast pace from start to finish, are anxious to begin their intellectual course gently and mildly. In any event, writing—the act of writing—is vital to almost any scheme. I would say it was vital to every scheme, without exception, were I not sure that some kind correspondent would instantly point out a scheme to which writing was obviously not vital.

After writing comes thinking. (The sequence may be considered odd, but I adhere to it.) In this connexion I cannot do better than quote an admirable letter which I have received from a correspondent who wishes to be known only as "An Oxford Lecturer." The italics (except the last) are mine, not his. He says: "Till a man has got his physical brain completely under his control—*suppressing its too-great receptivity, its tendencies to reproduce idly the thoughts of others, and to be swayed by every passing gust of emotion*—I hold that he cannot do a tenth part of the work that he would then be able to perform with little or no effort. Moreover, work apart, he has not entered upon his kingdom, and unlimited possibilities of future development are barred to him. Mental efficiency can be gained by constant practice in meditation—i.e., by concentrating the mind, say, for but ten minutes daily, but with absolute regularity, on some of the highest thoughts of which it is capable. Failures will be frequent, but they must be regarded with simple indifference and dogged perseverance in the path chosen. If that path be followed *without intermission* even for a few weeks the results will speak for themselves." I thoroughly agree with what this correspondent says, and am obliged to him for having so ably stated the case. But I regard such a practice of meditation as he indicates as being rather an "advanced" exercise for a beginner. After the beginner has got under way, and gained a little confidence in his strength of purpose, and acquired the skill to define his thoughts sufficiently to write them down—then it would be time enough, in my view, to undertake what "An Oxford Lecturer" suggests. By the way, he highly recommends Mrs. Annie Besant's book, *Thought Power: Its Control and Culture*. He says that it treats the subject with scientific clearness, and gives a practical method of training the mind, I endorse the latter part of the statement.

So much for the more or less technical processes of stirring the mind from its sloth and making it exactly obedient to the aspirations of the soul. And here I close. Numerous correspondents have asked me to outline a course of reading for them. In other words, they have asked me to particularize for them the aspirations of their souls. My subject, however, was not self-development My subject was mental efficiency as a means to self-development. Of course, one can only acquire mental efficiency in the actual effort of self-development. But I was concerned, not with the choice of route; rather with the manner of following the route. You say to me that I am busying myself with the best method of walking, and refusing to discuss where to go. Precisely. One man cannot tell another man where the other man wants to go.

If he can't himself decide on a goal he may as well curl up and expire, for the root of the matter is not in him. I will content myself with pointing out that the entire universe is open for inspection. Too many people fancy that self-development means literature. They associate the higher life with an intimate knowledge of the life of Charlotte Brontë, or the order of the plays of Shakespeare. The higher life may just as well be butterflies, or funeral customs, or county boundaries, or street names, or mosses, or stars, or slugs, as Charlotte Brontë or Shakespeare. Choose what interests you. Lots of finely-organized, mentally-efficient persons can't read Shakespeare at any price, and if you asked them who was the author of *The Tenant of Wildfell Hall* they might proudly answer Emily Brontë, if they didn't say they never heard of it. An accurate knowledge of *any* subject, coupled with a carefully nurtured sense of the relativity of that subject to other subjects, implies an enormous self-development. With this hint I conclude.

II

EXPRESSING ONE'S INDIVIDUALITY

A most curious and useful thing to realize is that one never knows the impression one is creating on other people. One may often guess pretty accurately whether it is good, bad, or indifferent—some people render it unnecessary for one to guess, they practically inform one—but that is not what I mean. I mean much more than that. I mean that one has one's self no mental picture corresponding to the mental picture which one's personality leaves in the minds of one's friends. Has it ever struck you that there is a mysterious individual going around, walking the streets, calling at houses for tea, chatting, laughing, grumbling, arguing, and that all your friends know him and have long since added him up and come to a definite conclusion about him—without saying more than a chance, cautious word to you; and that that person is *you*? Supposing that *you* came into a drawing-room where you were having tea, do you think you would recognize yourself as an individuality? I think not. You would be apt to say to yourself, as guests do when disturbed in drawing-rooms by other guests: "Who's this chap? Seems rather queer, I hope he won't be a bore." And your first telling would be slightly hostile. Why, even when you meet yourself in an unsuspected mirror in the very clothes that you have put on that very day and that you know by heart, you are almost always shocked by the realization that you are you. And now and then, when you have gone to the glass to arrange your hair in the full sobriety of early morning, have you not looked on an absolute stranger, and has not that stranger piqued your curiosity? And if it is thus with precise external details of form, colour, and movement, what may it not be with the vague complex effect of the mental and moral individuality?

A man honestly tries to make a good impression. What is the result? The result merely is that his friends, in the privacy of their minds, set him down as a man who tries to make a good impression. If much depends on the result of a single interview, or a couple of interviews, a man may conceivably force another to accept an impression of himself which he would like to convey. But if the receiver of the impression is to have time at his disposal, then the giver of the impression may just as well sit down and put his hands in his pockets, for nothing that he can do will modify or influence in any way the impression that he will ultimately give. The real impress is, in the end, given unconsciously, not consciously; and further, it is received unconsciously, not consciously. It depends partly on both persons. And it is immutably fixed beforehand. There can be no final deception. Take the extreme case, that of the mother and her son. One hears that the son hoodwinks his mother. Not he! If he is cruel, neglectful, overbearing, she is perfectly aware of it. He does not deceive her, and she does not deceive herself. I have often thought: If a son could look into a mother's heart, what an eye-opener he would have! "What!" he would cry. "This cold, impartial judgment, this keen vision for my faults, this implacable memory of little slights, and injustices, and callousnesses committed long ago, in the breast of my mother!" Yes, my friend, in the breast of your mother. The only difference between your mother and another person is that she takes you as you are, and loves you for what you are. She isn't blind: do not imagine it.

The marvel is, not that people are such bad judges of character, but that they are such good judges, especially of what I may call fundamental character. The wiliest person cannot for ever conceal his fundamental character from the simplest. And people are very stern judges, too. Think of your best friends— are you oblivious of their defects? On the contrary, you are perhaps too conscious of them. When you summon them before your mind's eye, it is no ideal creation that you see. When you meet them and talk to them you are constantly making reservations in their disfavour—unless, of course, you happen to be a schoolgirl gushing over like a fountain with enthusiasm. It is well, when one is judging a friend, to remember that he is judging you with the same godlike and superior impartiality. It is well to grasp the fact that you are going through life under the scrutiny of a band of acquaintances who are subject to very few illusions about you, whose views of you are, indeed, apt to be harsh and even cruel. Above all it is advisable to comprehend thoroughly that the things in your individuality which annoy your friends most are the things of which you are completely unconscious. It is not until years have passed that one begins to be able to form a dim idea of what one has looked like to one's friends. At forty one goes back ten years, and one says sadly, but with a certain amusement: "I must have been pretty blatant then. I can see how I must have exasperated 'em. And yet I hadn't the faintest notion of it at the time. My intentions were of the best. Only I didn't know enough." And one recollects some particularly crude action, and kicks one's self.... Yes, that is all very well; and the enlightenment which has come with increasing age is exceedingly satisfactory. But you are forty now. What shall you be saying of yourself at fifty? Such reflections foster humility, and they foster also a reluctance, which it is impossible to praise too highly, to tread on other people's toes.

A moment ago I used the phrase "fundamental character." It is a reminiscence of Stevenson's phrase "fundamental decency." And it is the final test by which one judges one's friends. "After all, he's a decent fellow." We must be able to use that formula concerning our friends. Kindliness of heart is not the greatest of human qualities—and its general effect on the progress of the world is not entirely beneficent—but it is the greatest of human qualities in friendship. It is the least dispensable quality. We come back to it with relief from more brilliant qualities. And it has the great advantage of always going with a broad mind. Narrow-minded people are never kind-hearted. You may be inclined to dispute this statement: please think it over; I am inclined to uphold it.

We can forgive the absence of any quality except kindliness of heart. And when a man lacks that, we blame him, we will not forgive him. This is, of course, scandalous. A man is born as he is born. And he can as easily add a cubit to his stature as add kindliness to his heart. The feat never has been done, and never will be done. And yet we blame those who have not kindliness. We have the incredible, insufferable, and odious audacity to blame them. We think of them as though they had nothing to do but go into a shop and buy kindliness. I hear you say that kindliness of heart can be "cultivated." Well, I hate to have even the appearance of contradicting you, but it can only be cultivated in the botanical sense. You can't cultivate violets on a nettle. A philosopher has enjoined us to suffer fools gladly. He had more usefully enjoined us to suffer ill-natured persons gladly.... I see that in a fit of absentmindedness I have strayed into the pulpit. I descend.

III

BREAKING WITH THE PAST

On that dark morning we woke up, and it instantly occurred to us—or at any rate to those of us who have preserved some of our illusions and our *naïveté*—that we had something to be cheerful about, some cause for a gay and strenuous vivacity; and then we remembered that it was New Year's Day, and there were those Resolutions to put into force! Of course, we all smile in a superior manner at the very mention of New Year's Resolutions; we pretend they are toys for children, and that we have long since ceased to regard them seriously as a possible aid to conduct. But we are such deceivers, such miserable, moral cowards, in such terror of appearing naïve, that I for one am not to be taken in by that smile and that pretence. The individual who scoffs at New Year's Resolutions resembles the woman who says she doesn't look under the bed at nights; the truth is not in him, and in the very moment of his lying, could his cranium suddenly become transparent, we should see Resolutions burning brightly in his brain like lamps in Trafalgar Square. Of this I am convinced, that nineteen-twentieths of us got out of bed that morning animated by that special feeling of gay and strenuous vivacity which Resolutions alone can produce. And nineteen-twentieths of us were also conscious of a high virtue, forgetting that it is not the making of Resolutions, but the keeping of them, which renders pardonable the consciousness of virtue.

And at this hour, while the activity of the Resolution is yet in full blast, I would wish to insist on the truism, obvious perhaps, but apt to be overlooked, that a man cannot go forward and stand still at the same time. Just as moralists have often animadverted upon the tendency to live in the future, so I would animadvert upon the tendency to live in the past. Because all around me I see men carefully tying themselves with an unbreakable rope to an immovable post at the bottom of a hill and then struggling to climb the hill. If there is one Resolution more important than another it is the Resolution to break with the past. If life is not a continual denial of the past, then it is nothing. This may seem a hard and callous doctrine, but you know there are aspects of common sense which decidedly are hard and callous. And one finds constantly in plain common-sense persons (O rare and select band!) a surprising quality of ruthlessness mingled with softer traits. Have you not noticed it? The past is absolutely intractable. One can't do anything with it. And an exaggerated attention to it is like an exaggerated attention to sepulchres—a sign of barbarism. Moreover, the past is usually the enemy of cheerfulness, and cheerfulness is a most precious attainment.

Personally, I could even go so far as to exhibit hostility towards grief, and a marked hostility towards remorse—two states of mind which feed on the past instead of on the present. Remorse, which is not the same thing as repentance, serves no purpose that I have ever been able to discover. What one has done, one has done, and there's an end of it. As a great prelate unforgettably said, "Things are what they are, and the consequences of them will be what they will be. Why, then, attempt to deceive ourselves"—that remorse for wickedness is a useful and praiseworthy exercise? Much better to forget. As a matter of fact, people "indulge" in remorse; it is a somewhat vicious form of spiritual pleasure. Grief, of course, is different, and it must be handled with delicate consideration. Nevertheless, when I see, as one does see, a man or a woman dedicating existence to sorrow for the loss of a beloved creature, and the world tacitly applauding, my feeling is certainly inimical. To my idea, that man or woman is not honouring, but dishonouring, the memory of the departed; society suffers, the individual suffers, and no earthly or heavenly good is achieved. Grief is of the past; it mars the present; it is a form of indulgence, and it ought to be bridled much more than it often is. The human heart is so large that mere remembrance should not be allowed to tyrannize over every part of it.

But cases of remorse and absorbing grief are comparatively rare. What is not rare is that misguided loyalty to the past which dominates the lives of so many of us. I do not speak of leading principles, which are not likely to incommode us by changing; I speak of secondary yet still important things. We will not do so-

and-so because we have never done it—as if that was a reason! Or we have always done so-and-so, therefore we must always do it—as if *that* was logic! This disposition to an irrational Toryism is curiously discoverable in advanced Radicals, and it will show itself in the veriest trifles. I remember such a man whose wife objected to his form of hat (not that I would call so crowning an affair as a hat a trifle!). "My dear," he protested, "I have always worn this sort of hat. It may not suit me, but it is absolutely impossible for me to alter it now." However, she took him by means of an omnibus to a hat shop and bought him another hat and put it on his head, and made a present of the old one to the shop assistant, and marched him out of the shop. "There!" she said, "you see how impossible it is." This is a parable. And I will not insult your intelligence by applying it.

The faculty that we chiefly need when we are in the resolution-making mood is the faculty of imagination, the faculty of looking at our lives as though we had never looked at them before—freshly, with a new eye. Supposing that you had been born mature and full of experience, and that yesterday had been the first day of your life, you would regard it to-day as an experiment, you would challenge each act in it, and you would probably arrange to-morrow in a manner that showed a healthy disrespect for yesterday. You certainly would not say: "I have done so-and-so once, therefore I must keep on doing it." The past is never more than an experiment. A genuine appreciation of this fact will make our new Resolutions more valuable and drastic than they usually are. I have a dim notion that the most useful Resolution for most of us would be to break quite fifty per cent. of all the vows we have ever made. "Do not accustom yourself to enchain your *volatility* with vows…. Take this warning; it is of great importance." (The wisdom is Johnson's, but I flatter myself on the italics.)

IV

SETTLING DOWN IN LIFE

The other day a well-known English novelist asked me how old I thought she was, *really*. "Well," I said to myself, "since she has asked for it, she shall have it; I will be as true to life as her novels." So I replied audaciously: "Thirty-eight." I fancied I was erring if at all, on the side of "really," and I trembled. She laughed triumphantly. "I am forty-three," she said. The incident might have passed off entirely to my satisfaction had she not proceeded: "And now tell me how old *you* are." That was like a woman. Women imagine that men have no reticences, no pretty little vanities. What an error! Of course I could not be beaten in candour by a woman. I had to offer myself a burnt sacrifice to her curiosity, and I did it, bravely but not unflinchingly. And then afterwards the fact of my age remained with me, worried me, obsessed me. I saw more clearly than ever before that age was telling on me. I could not be blind to the deliberation of my movements in climbing stairs and in dressing. Once upon a time the majority of persons I met in the street seemed much older than myself. It is different now. The change has come unperceived. There is a generation younger than mine that smokes cigars and falls in love. Astounding! Once I could play left-wing forward for an hour and a half without dropping down dead. Once I could swim a hundred and fifty feet submerged at the bottom of a swimming-bath. Incredible! Simply incredible!... Can it be that I have already lived?

And lo! I, at the age of nearly forty, am putting to myself the old questions concerning the intrinsic value of life, the fundamentally important questions: What have I got out of it? What am I likely to get out of it? In a word, what's it worth? If a man can ask himself a question more momentous, radical, and critical than these questions, I would like to know what it is. Innumerable philosophers have tried to answer these questions in a general way for the average individual, and possibly they have succeeded pretty well. Possibly I might derive benefit from a perusal of their answers. But do you suppose I am going to read them? Not I! Do you suppose that I can recall the wisdom that I happen already to have read? Not I! My mind is a perfect blank at this moment in regard to the wisdom of others on the essential question. Strange, is it not? But quite a common experience, I believe. Besides, I don't actually care twopence what any other philosopher has replied to my question. In this, each man must be his own philosopher. There is an instinct in the profound egoism of human nature which prevents us from accepting such ready-made answers. What is it to us what Plato thought? Nothing. And thus the question remains ever new, and ever unanswered, and ever of dramatic interest. The singular, the highly singular thing is— and here I arrive at my point—that so few people put the question to themselves in time, that so many put it too late, or even die without putting it.

I am firmly convinced that an immense proportion of my instructed fellow-creatures do not merely omit to strike the balance-sheet of their lives, they omit even the preliminary operation of taking stock. They go on, and on, and on, buying and selling they know not what, at unascertained prices, dropping money into the till and taking it out. They don't know what goods are in the shop, nor what amount is in the till, but they have a clear impression that the living-room behind the shop is by no means as luxurious and as well-ventilated as they would like it to be. And the years pass, and that beautiful furniture and that system of ventilation are not achieved. And then one day they die, and friends come to the funeral and remark: "Dear me! How stuffy this room is, and the shop's practically full of trash!" Or, some little time before they are dead, they stay later than usual in the shop one evening, and make up their minds to take stock and count the till, and the disillusion lays them low, and they struggle into the living-room and murmur: "I shall never have that beautiful furniture, and I shall never have that system of ventilation. If I had known earlier, I would have at least got a few inexpensive cushions to go on with, and I would have put my fist through a pane in the window. But it's too late now. I'm used to Windsor chairs, and I should feel the draught horribly."

If I were a preacher, and if I hadn't got more than enough to do in minding my own affairs, and if I could look any one in the face and deny that I too had pursued for nearly forty years the great British policy of muddling through and hoping for the best—in short, if things were not what they are, I would hire the Alhambra Theatre or Exeter Hall of a Sunday night—preferably the Alhambra, because more people would come to my entertainment—and I would invite all men and women over twenty-six. I would supply the seething crowd with what they desired in the way of bodily refreshment (except spirits—I would draw the line at poisons), and having got them and myself into a nice amiable expansive frame of mind, I would thus address them—of course in ringing eloquence that John Bright might have envied:

Men and women (I would say), companions in the universal pastime of hiding one's head in the sand,—I am about to impart to you the very essence of human wisdom. It is not abstract. It is a principle of daily application, affecting the daily round in its entirety, from the straphanging on the District Railway in the morning to the straphanging on the District Railway the next morning. Beware of hope, and beware of ambition! Each is excellently tonic, like German competition, in moderation. But all of you are suffering from self-indulgence in the first, and very many of you are ruining your constitutions with the second. Be it known unto you, my dear men and women, that existence rightly considered is a fair compromise between two instincts—the instinct of hoping one day to live, and the instinct to live here and now. In most of you the first instinct has simply got the other by the throat and is throttling it. Prepare to live by all means, but for heaven's sake do not forget to live. You will never have a better chance than you have at present. You may think you will have, but you are mistaken. Pardon this bluntness. Surely you are not so naïve as to imagine that the road on the other side of that hill there is more beautiful than the piece you are now traversing! Hopes are never realized; for in the act of realization they become something else. Ambitions may be attained, but ambitions attained are rather like burnt coal, ninety per cent. of the heat generated has gone up the chimney instead of into the room. Nevertheless, indulge in hopes and ambitions, which, though deceiving, are agreeable deceptions; let them cheat you a little, a lot. But do not let them cheat you too much. This that you are living now is life itself—it is much more life itself than that which you will be living twenty years hence. Grasp that truth. Dwell on it. Absorb it. Let it influence your conduct, to the end that neither the present nor the future be neglected. You search for happiness? Happiness is chiefly a matter of temperament. It is exceedingly improbable that you will by struggling gain more happiness than you already possess. In fine, settle down at once into life. (Loud cheers.)

The cheers would of course be for the refreshments.

There is no doubt that the mass of the audience would consider that I had missed my vocation, and ought to have been a caterer instead of a preacher. But, once started, I would not be discouraged. I would keep on, Sunday night after Sunday night. Our leading advertisers have richly proved that the public will believe anything if they are told of it often enough. I would practise iteration, always with refreshments. In the result, it would dawn upon the corporate mind that there was some glimmering of sense in my doctrine, and people would at last begin to perceive the folly of neglecting to savour the present, the folly of assuming that the future can be essentially different from the present, the fatuity of dying before they have begun to live.

V

MARRIAGE

THE DUTY OF IT

Every now and then it becomes necessary to deal faithfully with that immortal type of person, the praiser of the past at the expense of the present. I will not quote Horace, as by all the traditions of letters I ought to do, because Horace, like the incurable trimmer that he was, "hedged" on this question; and I do not admire him much either. The praiser of the past has been very rife lately. He has told us that pauperism and lunacy are mightily increasing, and though the exact opposite has been proved to be the case and he has apologized, he will have forgotten the correction in a few months, and will break out again into renewed lamentation. He has told us that we are physically deteriorating, and in such awful tones that we have shuddered, and many of us have believed. And considering that the death-rate is decreasing, that slums are decreasing, that disease is decreasing, that the agricultural labourer eats more than ever he did, our credence does not do much credit to our reasoning powers, does it? Of course, there is that terrible "influx" into the towns, but I for one should be much interested to know wherein the existence of the rustic in times past was healthier than the existence of the town-dwellers of to-day. The personal appearance of agricultural veterans does not help me; they resemble starved 'bus-drivers twisted out of shape by lightning.

But the *pièce de résistance* of the praiser of the past is now marriage, with discreet hints about the birth-rate. The praiser of the past is going to have a magnificent time with the subject of marriage. The first moanings of the tempest have already been heard. Bishops have looked askance at the birth-rate, and have mentioned their displeasure. The matter is serious. As the phrase goes, "it strikes at the root." We are marrying later, my friends. Some of us, in the hurry and pre-occupation of business, are quite forgetting to marry. It is the duty of the citizen to marry and have children, and we are neglecting our duty, we are growing selfish! No longer are produced the glorious "quiverfuls" of old times! Our fathers married at twenty; we marry at thirty-five. Why? Because a gross and enervating luxury has overtaken us. What will become of England if this continues? There will be no England! Hence we must look to it! And so on, in the same strain.

I should like to ask all those who have raised and will raise such outcries. Have you read "X"? Now, the book that I refer to as "X" is a mysterious work, written rather more than a hundred years ago by an English curate. It is a classic of English science; indeed, it is one of the great scientific books of the world. It has immensely influenced all the scientific thought of the nineteenth century, especially Darwin's. Mr. H.G. Wells, as cited in "Chambers's Cyclopædia of English Literature," describes it as "the most 'shattering' book that ever has or will be written." If I may make a personal reference, I would say that it affected me more deeply than any other scientific book that I have read. Although it is perfectly easy to understand, and free from the slightest technicality, it is the most misunderstood book in English literature, simply because it is *not* read. The current notion about it is utterly false. It might be a powerful instrument of education, general and sociological, but publishers will not reprint it—at least, they do not. And yet it is forty times more interesting and four hundred times more educational than Gilbert White's remarks on the birds of Selborne. I will leave you to guess what "X" is, but I do not offer a prize for the solution of a problem which a vast number of my readers will certainly solve at once.

If those who are worrying themselves about the change in our system of marriage would read "X," they would probably cease from worrying. For they would perceive that they had been putting the cart before the horse; that they had elevated to the dignity of fundamental principles certain average rules of conduct which had sprung solely from certain average instincts in certain average conditions, and that they were now frightened because, the conditions having changed, the rules of conduct had changed with them. One of the truths that "X" makes clear is that conduct conforms to conditions, and not conditions to conduct.

The payment of taxes is a duty which the citizen owes to the state. Marriage, with the begetting of children, is not a duty which the citizen owes to the state. Marriage, with its consequences, is a matter of personal inclination and convenience. It never has been anything else, and it never will be anything else. How could it be otherwise? If a man goes against inclination and convenience in a matter where inclination is "of the essence of the contract," he merely presents the state with a discontented citizen (if not two) in exchange for a contented one! The happiness of the state is the sum of the happiness of all its citizens; to decrease one's own happiness, then, is a singular way of doing one's duty to the state! Do you imagine that when people married early and much they did so from a sense of duty to the state—a sense of duty which our "modern luxury" has weakened? I imagine they married simply because it suited 'em. They married from sheer selfishness, as all decent people do marry. And do those who clatter about the duty of marriage kiss the girls of their hearts with an eye to the general welfare? I can fancy them saying, "My angel, I love you—from a sense of duty to the state. Let us rear innumerable progeny—from a sense of duty to the state." How charmed the girls would be!

If the marrying age changes, if the birth-rate shows a sympathetic tendency to follow the death-rate (as it must—see "X"), no one need be alarmed. Elementary principles of right and wrong are not trembling on their bases. The human conscience is not silenced. The nation is not going to the dogs. Conduct is adjusting itself to new conditions, and that is all. We may not be able to see exactly *how* conditions are changing; that is a detail; our descendants will see exactly; meanwhile the change in our conduct affords us some clew. And although certain nervous persons do get alarmed, and do preach, and do "take measures," the rest of us may remain placid in the sure faith that "measures" will avail nothing whatever. If there are two things set high above legislation, "movements," crusades, and preaching, one is the marrying age and the other is the birth-rate. For there the supreme instinct comes along and stamps ruthlessly on all insincere reasonings and sham altruisms; stamps on everything, in fact, and blandly remarks: "I shall suit my own convenience, and no one but Nature herself (with a big, big N) shall talk to *me*. Don't pester me with Right and Wrong. I *am* Right and Wrong...." Having thus attempted to clear the ground a little of fudge, I propose next to offer a few simple remarks on marriage.

THE ADVENTURE OF IT

Having endeavoured to show that men do not, and should not, marry from a sense of duty to the state or to mankind, but simply and solely from an egoistic inclination to marry, I now proceed to the individual case of the man who is "in a position to marry" and whose affections are not employed. Of course, if he has fallen in love, unless he happens to be a person of extremely powerful will, he will not weigh the pros and cons of marriage; he will merely marry, and forty thousand cons will not prevent him. And he will be absolutely right and justified, just as the straw as it rushes down the current is absolutely right and justified. But the privilege of falling in love is not given to everybody, and the inestimable privilege of falling deeply in love is given to few. However, the man whom circumstances permit to marry but who is not in love, or is only slightly amorous, will still think of marriage. How will he think of it?

I will tell you. In the first place, if he has reached the age of thirty unscathed by Aphrodite, he will reflect that that peculiar feeling of romantic expectation with which he gets up every morning would cease to exist after marriage—and it is a highly agreeable feeling! In its stead, in moments of depression, he would have the feeling of having done something irremediable, of having definitely closed an avenue for the outlet of his individuality. (Kindly remember that I am not describing what this human man ought to think. I am describing what he does think.) In the second place, he will reflect that, after marriage, he could no longer expect the charming welcomes which bachelors so often receive from women; he would be "done with" as a possibility, and he does not relish the prospect of being done with as a possibility. Such considerations, all connected more or less with the loss of "freedom" (oh, mysterious and thrilling word!), will affect his theoretical attitude. And be it known that even the freedom to be lonely and melancholy is still freedom.

Other ideas will suggest themselves. One morning while brushing his hair he will see a gray hair, and, however young he may be, the anticipation of old age will come to him. A solitary old age! A senility dependent for its social and domestic requirements on condescending nephews and nieces, or even more distant relations! Awful! Unthinkable! And his first movement, especially if he has read that terrible novel, "*Fort comme la Mort*," of De Maupassant, is to rush out into the street and propose to the first girl he encounters, in order to avoid this dreadful nightmare of a solitary old age. But before he has got as far as the doorstep he reflects further. Suppose he marries, and after twenty years his wife dies and leaves him a widower! He will still have a solitary old age, and a vastly more tragical one than if he had remained single. Marriage is not, therefore, a sure remedy for a solitary old age; it may intensify the evil. Children? But suppose he doesn't have any children! Suppose, there being children, they die—what anguish! Suppose merely that they are seriously ill and recover—what an ageing experience! Suppose they prove a disappointment— what endless regret! Suppose they "turn out badly" (children do)—what shame! Suppose he finally becomes dependent upon the grudging kindness of an ungrateful child—what a supreme humiliation! All these things are occurring constantly everywhere. Suppose his wife, having loved him, ceased to love him, or suppose he ceased to love his wife! *Ces choses ne se commandent pas*—these things do not command themselves. Personally, I should estimate that in not one per cent. even of romantic marriages are the husband and wife capable of *passion* for each other after three years. So brief is the violence of love! In perhaps thirty-three per cent. passion settles down into a tranquil affection—which is ideal. In fifty per cent. it sinks into sheer indifference, and one becomes used to one's wife or one's husband as to one's other habits. And in the remaining sixteen per cent. it develops into dislike or detestation. Do you think my percentages are wrong, you who have been married a long time and know what the world is? Well, you may modify them a little—you won't want to modify them much.

The risk of finding one's self ultimately among the sixteen per cent. can be avoided by the simple expedient of not marrying. And by the same expedient the other risks can be avoided, together with yet others that I have not mentioned. It is entirely obvious, then (in fact, I beg pardon for mentioning it), that the attitude towards marriage of the heart-free bachelor must be at best a highly cautious attitude. He knows he is already in the frying-pan (none knows better), but, considering the propinquity of the fire, he doubts whether he had not better stay where he is. His life will be calmer, more like that of a hibernating snake; his sensibilities will be dulled; but the chances of poignant suffering will be very materially reduced.

So that the bachelor in a position to marry but not in love will assuredly decide in theory against marriage—that is to say, if he is timid, if he prefers frying-pans, if he is lacking in initiative, if he has the soul of a rat, if he wants to live as little as possible, if he hates his kind, if his egoism is of the miserable sort that dares not mingle with another's. But if he has been more happily gifted he will decide that the magnificent adventure is worth plunging into; the ineradicable and fine gambling instinct in him will urge him to take, at the first chance, a ticket in the only lottery permitted by the British Government. Because, after all, the mutual sense of ownership felt by the normal husband and the normal wife is something unique, something the like of which cannot be obtained without marriage. I saw a man and a woman at a sale the other day; I was too far off to hear them, but I could perceive they were having a most lively argument—perhaps it was only about initials on pillowcases; they were *absorbed* in themselves; the world did not exist for them. And I thought: "What miraculous exquisite Force is it that brings together that strange, sombre, laconic organism in a silk hat and a loose, black overcoat, and that strange, bright, vivacious, querulous, irrational organism in brilliant fur and feathers?" And when they moved away the most interesting phenomenon in the universe moved away. And I thought: "Just as no beer is bad, but some beer is better than other beer, so no marriage is bad." The chief reward of marriage is something which marriage is bound to give— companionship whose mysterious *interestingness* nothing can stale. A man may hate his wife so that she can't thread a needle without annoying him, but when he dies, or she dies, he will say: "Well, *I was interested.*" And one always is. Said a bachelor of forty-six to me the other night: "Anything is better than the void."

THE TWO WAYS OF IT

Sabine and other summary methods of marrying being now abandoned by all nice people, there remain two broad general ways. The first is the English way. We let nature take her course. We give heed to the heart's cry. When, amid the hazards and accidents of the world, two souls "find each other," we rejoice. Our instinctive wish is that they shall marry, if the matter can anyhow be arranged. We frankly recognise the claim of romance in life, and we are prepared to make sacrifices to it. We see a young couple at the altar; they are in love. Good! They are poor. So much the worse! But nevertheless we feel that love will pull them through. The revolting French system of bargain and barter is the one thing that we can neither comprehend nor pardon in the customs of our great neighbours. We endeavour to be polite about that system; we simply cannot. It shocks our finest, tenderest feelings. It is so obviously contrary to nature.

The second is the French way, just alluded to as bargain and barter. Now, if there is one thing a Frenchman can neither comprehend nor pardon in the customs of a race so marvellously practical and sagacious as ourselves, it is the English marriage system. He endeavours to be polite about it, and he succeeds. But it shocks his finest, tenderest feelings. He admits that it is in accordance with nature; but he is apt to argue that the whole progress of civilisation has been the result of an effort to get away from nature. "What! Leave the most important relation into which a man can enter to the mercy of chance, when a mere gesture may arouse passion, or the colour of a corsage induce desire! No, you English, you who are so self-controlled, you are not going seriously to defend that! You talk of love as though it lasted for ever. You talk of sacrificing to love; but what you really sacrifice, or risk sacrificing, is the whole of the latter part of married existence for the sake of the first two or three years. Marriage is not one long honeymoon. We wish it were. When *you* agree to a marriage you fix your eyes on the honeymoon. When *we* agree to a marriage we try to see it as it will be five or ten years hence. We assert that, in the average instance, five years after the wedding it doesn't matter whether or not the parties were in love on the wedding-day. Hence we will not yield to the gusts of the moment. Your system is, moreover, if we may be permitted the observation, a premium on improvidence; it is, to some extent, the result of improvidence. You can marry your daughters without dowries, and the ability to do so tempts you to neglect your plain duty to your daughters, and you do not always resist the temptation. Do your marriages of 'romance' turn out better than our marriages of prudence, of careful thought, of long foresight? We do not think they do."

So much for the two ways. Patriotism being the last refuge of a scoundrel, according to Doctor Johnson, I have no intention of judging between them, as my heart prompts me to do, lest I should be accused of it. Nevertheless, I may hint that, while perfectly convinced by the admirable logic of the French, I am still, with the charming illogicalness of the English, in favour of romantic marriages (it being, of course, understood that dowries *ought* to be far more plentiful than they are in England). If a Frenchman accuses me of being ready to risk sacrificing the whole of the latter part of married life for the sake of the first two or three years, I would unhesitatingly reply: "Yes, I *am* ready to risk that sacrifice. I reckon the first two or three years are worth it." But, then, I am English, and therefore romantic by nature. Look at London, that city whose outstanding quality is its romantic quality; and look at the Englishwomen going their ways in the wonderful streets thereof! Their very eyes are full of romance. They may, they do, lack *chic*, but they are heroines of drama. Then look at Paris; there is little romance in the fine right lines of Paris. Look at the Parisiennes. They are the most astounding and adorable women yet invented by nature. But they aren't romantic, you know. They don't know what romance is. They are so matter-of-fact that when you think of their matter-of-factness it gives you a shiver in the small of your back.

To return. One may view the two ways in another light. Perhaps the difference between them is, fundamentally, less a difference between the ideas of two races than a difference between the ideas of two "times of life"; and in France the elderly attitude predominates. As people get on in years, even English people, they are more and more in favour of the marriage of reason as against the marriage of romance. Young people, even French people, object strongly to the theory and practice of the marriage of reason. But with them the unique and precious ecstasy of youth is not past, whereas their elders have forgotten its savour. Which is right? No one will ever be able to decide. But neither the one system nor the other will apply itself well to all or nearly all cases. There have been thousands of romantic marriages in England of which it may be said that it would have been better had the French system been in force to prevent their existence. And, equally, thousands of possible romantic marriages have been prevented in France which, had the English system prevailed there, would have turned out excellently. The prevalence of dowries in England would not render the English system perfect (for it must be remembered that money is only one of several ingredients in the French marriage), but it would considerably improve it. However, we are not a provident race, and we are not likely to become one. So our young men must reconcile themselves to the continued absence of dowries.

The reader may be excused for imagining that I am at the end of my remarks. I am not. All that precedes is a mere preliminary to what follows. I want to regard the case of the man who has given the English system a fair trial and found it futile. Thus, we wait on chance in England. We wait for love to arrive. Suppose it doesn't arrive? Where is the English system then? Assume that a man in a position to marry reaches thirty-five or forty without having fallen in love. Why should he not try the French system for a change? Any marriage is better than none at all. Naturally, in England, he couldn't go up to the Chosen Fair and announce: "I am not precisely in love with you, but will you marry me?" He would put it differently. And she would understand. And do you think she would refuse?

VI

BOOKS

THE PHYSICAL SIDE

The chief interest of many of my readers is avowedly books; they may, they probably do, profess other interests, but they are primarily "bookmen," and when one is a bookman one is a bookman during about twenty-three and three-quarter hours in every day. Now, bookmen are capable of understanding things about books which cannot be put into words; they are not like mere subscribers to circulating libraries; for them a book is not just a book—it is a *book*. If these lines should happen to catch the eye of any persons not bookmen, such persons may imagine that I am writing nonsense; but I trust that the bookmen will comprehend me. And I venture, then, to offer a few reflections upon an aspect of modern bookishness that is becoming more and more "actual" as the enterprise of publishers and the beneficent effects of education grow and increase together. I refer to "popular editions" of classics.

Now, I am very grateful to the devisers of cheap and handy editions. The first book I ever bought was the first volume of the first modern series of presentable and really cheap reprints, namely, Macaulay's "Warren Hastings," in "Cassell's National Library" (sixpence, in cloth). That foundation stone of my library has unfortunately disappeared beneath the successive deposits, but another volume of the same series, F.T. Palgrave's "Visions of England" (an otherwise scarce book), still remains to me through the vicissitudes of seventeen years of sale, purchase, and exchange, and I would not care to part with it. I have over two hundred volumes of that inestimable and incomparable series, "The Temple Classics," besides several hundred assorted volumes of various other series. And when I heard of the new "Everyman's Library," projected by that benefactor of bookmen, Mr. J.M. Dent, my first impassioned act was to sit down and write a postcard to my bookseller ordering George Finlay's "The Byzantine Empire," a work which has waited sixty years for popular recognition. So that I cannot be said to be really antagonistic to cheap reprints.

Strong in this consciousness, I beg to state that cheap and handy reprints are "all very well in their way"—which is a manner of saying that they are not the Alpha and Omega of bookishness. By expending £20 yearly during the next five years a man might collect, in cheap and handy reprints, all that was worth having in classic English literature. But I for one would not be willing to regard such a library as a real library. I would regard it as only a cheap edition of a library. There would be something about it that would arouse in me a certain benevolent disdain, even though every volume was well printed on good paper and inoffensively bound. Why? Well, although it is my profession in life to say what I feel in plain words, I do not know that in this connection I *can* say what I feel in plain words. I have to rely on a sympathetic comprehension of my attitude in the bookish breasts of my readers.

In the first place, I have an instinctive antipathy to a "series." I do not want "The Golden Legend" and "The Essays of Elia" uniformed alike in a regiment of books. It makes me think of conscription and barracks. Even the noblest series of reprints ever planned (not at all cheap, either, nor heterogeneous in matter), the Tudor Translations, faintly annoys me in the mass. Its appearances in a series seems to me to rob a book of something very delicate and subtle in the aroma of its individuality—something which, it being inexplicable, I will not try to explain.

In the second place, most cheap and handy reprints are small in size. They may be typographically excellent, with large type and opaque paper; they may be convenient to handle; they may be surpassingly suitable for the pocket and the very thing for travel; they may save precious space where shelf-room is limited; but they are small in size. And there is, as regards most literature, a distinct moral value in size. Do I carry my audience with me? I hope so. Let "Paradise Lost" be so produced that you can put it in your waistcoat pocket, and it is no more "Paradise Lost." Milton needs a solid octavo form, with stoutish paper and long primer type. I have "Walpole's Letters" in Newnes's "Thin Paper Classics," a marvellous volume of near nine hundred pages, with a portrait and a good index and a beautiful binding, for three and six, and I am exceedingly indebted to Messrs. Newnes for creating that volume. It was sheer genius on their part to do so. I get charming sensations from it, but sensations not so charming as I should get from Mrs. Paget Toynbee's many-volumed and grandiose edition, even aside from Mrs. Toynbee's erudite notes and the extra letters which she has been able to print. The same letter in Mrs. Toynbee's edition would have a higher æsthetic and moral value for me than in the "editionlet" of Messrs. Newnes. The one cheap series which satisfies my desire for size is Macmillan's "Library of English Classics," in which I have the "Travels" of that mythical personage, Sir John Mandeville. But it is only in paying for it that you know this edition to be cheap, for it measures nine inches by six inches by two inches.

And in the third place, when one buys series, one only partially chooses one's books; they are mainly chosen for one by the publisher. And even if they are not chosen for one by the publisher, they are suggested *to* one by the publisher. Not so does the genuine bookman form his library. The genuine bookman begins by having specific desires. His study of authorities gives him a demand, and the demand forces him to find the supply. He does not let the supply create the demand. Such a state of affairs would be almost humiliating, almost like the *parvenu* who calls in the wholesale furnisher and decorator to provide him with a home. A library must be, primarily, the expression of the owner's personality.

Let me assert again that I am strongly in favour of cheap series of reprints. Their influence though not the very finest, is undisputably good. They are as great a boon as cheap bread. They are indispensable where money or space is limited, and in travelling. They decidedly help to educate a taste for books that are neither cheap nor handy; and the most luxurious collectors may not afford to ignore them entirely. But they have their limitations, their disadvantages. They cannot form the backbone of a "proper" library. They make, however, admirable embroidery to a library. My own would look rather plain if it was stripped of them.

THE PHILOSOPHY OF BOOK-BUYING

For some considerable time I have been living, as regards books, with the minimum of comfort and decency—with, in fact, the bare necessaries of life, such necessaries being, in my case, sundry dictionaries, Boswell, an atlas, Wordsworth, an encyclopædia, Shakespere, Whitaker, some De Maupassant, a poetical anthology, Verlaine, Baudelaire, a natural history of my native county, an old directory of my native town, Sir Thomas Browne, Poe, Walpole's Letters, and a book of memoirs that I will not name. A curious list, you will say. Well, never mind! We do not all care to eat beefsteak and chip potatoes off an oak table, with a foaming quart to the right hand. We have our idiosyncrasies. The point is that I existed on the bare necessaries of life (very healthy—doctors say) for a long time. And then, just lately, I summoned energy and caused fifteen hundred volumes to be transported to me; and I arranged them on shelves; and I re-arranged them on shelves; and I left them to arrange themselves on shelves.

Well, you know, the way that I walk up and down in front of these volumes, whose faces I had half-forgotten, is perfectly infantile. It is like the way of a child at a menagerie. There, in its cage, is that 1839 edition of Shelley, edited by Mrs. Shelley, that I once nearly sold to the British Museum because the Keeper of Printed Books thought he hadn't got a copy—only he had! And there, in a cage by himself, because of his terrible hugeness, is the 1652 Paris edition of Montaigne's Essays. And so I might continue, and so I would continue, were it not essential that I come to my argument.

Do you suppose that the presence of these books, after our long separation, is making me read more than I did? Do you suppose I am engaged in looking up my favourite passages? Not a bit. The other evening I had a long tram journey, and, before starting, I tried to select a book to take with me. I couldn't find one to suit just the tram-mood. As I had to *catch* the tram I was obliged to settle on something, and in the end I went off with nothing more original than "Hamlet," which I am really too familiar with…. Then I bought an evening paper, and read it all through, including advertisements. So I said to myself: "This is a nice result of all my trouble to resume company with some of my books!" However, as I have long since ceased to be surprised at the eccentric manner in which human nature refuses to act as one would have expected it to act, I was able to keep calm and unashamed during this extraordinary experience. And I am still walking up and down in front of my books and enjoying them without reading them.

I wish to argue that a great deal of cant is talked (and written) about reading. Papers such as the "Anthenæum," which nevertheless I peruse with joy from end to end every week, can scarcely notice a new edition of a classic without expressing, in a grieved and pessimistic tone, the fear that more people buy these agreeable editions than read them. And if it is so? What then? Are we only to buy the books that we read? The question has merely to be thus bluntly put, and it answers itself. All impassioned bookmen, except a few who devote their whole lives to reading, have rows of books on their shelves which they have never read, and which they never will read. I know that I have hundreds such. My eye rests on the works of Berkeley in three volumes, with a preface by the Right Honourable Arthur James Balfour. I cannot conceive the circumstances under which I shall ever read Berkeley; but I do not regret having bought him in a good edition, and I would buy him again if I had him not; for when I look at him some of his virtue passes into me; I am the better for him. A certain aroma of philosophy informs my soul, and I am less crude than I should otherwise be. This is not fancy, but fact.

Taking Berkeley simply as an instance, I will utilise him a little further. I ought to have read Berkeley, you say; just as I ought to have read Spenser, Ben Jonson, George Eliot, Victor Hugo. Not at all. There is no "ought" about it. If the mass of obtainable first-class literature were, as it was perhaps a century ago, not too large to be assimilated by a man of ordinary limited leisure *in* his leisure and during the first half of his life, then possibly there might be an "ought" about it. But the mass has grown unmanageable, even by those robust professional readers who can "grapple with whole libraries." And I am not a professional reader. I am a writer, just as I might be a hotel-keeper, a solicitor, a doctor, a grocer, or an earthenware manufacturer. I read in my scanty spare time, and I don't read in all my spare time, either. I have other distractions. I read what I feel inclined to read, and I am conscious of no duty to finish a book that I don't care to finish. I read in my leisure, not from a sense of duty, not to improve myself, but solely because it gives me pleasure to read. Sometimes it takes me a month to get through one book. I expect my case is quite an average case. But am I going to fetter my buying to my reading? Not exactly! I want to have lots of books on my shelves because I know they are good, because I know they would amuse me, because I like to look at them, and because one day I might have a caprice to read them. (Berkeley, even thy turn may come!) In short, I want them because I want them. And shall I be deterred from possessing them by the fear of some sequestered and singular person, some person who has read vastly but who doesn't know the difference between a J.S. Muria cigar and an R.P. Muria, strolling in and bullying me with the dreadful query: "*Sir, do you read your books?*"

Therefore I say: In buying a book, be influenced by two considerations only. Are you reasonably sure that it is a good book? Have you a desire to possess it? Do not be influenced by the probability or the improbability of your reading it. After all, one does read a certain proportion of what one buys. And further, instinct counts. The man who spends half a crown on Stubbs's "Early Plantagenets" instead of going into the Gaiety pit to see "The Spring Chicken," will probably be the sort of man who can suck goodness out of Stubbs's "Early Plantagenets" years before he bestirs himself to read it.

VII

SUCCESS

CANDID REMARKS

There are times when the whole free and enlightened Press of the United Kingdom seems to become strangely interested in the subject of "success," of getting on in life. We are passing through such a period now. It would be difficult to name the prominent journalists who have not lately written, in some form or another, about success. Most singular phenomenon of all, Dr. Emil Reich has left Plato, duchesses, and Claridge's Hotel, in order to instruct the million readers of a morning paper in the principles of success! What the million readers thought of the Doctor's stirring and strenuous sentences I will not imagine; but I know what I thought, as a plain man. After taking due cognizance of his airy play with the "constants" and "variables" of success, after watching him treat "energetics" (his wonderful new name for the "science" of success) as though because he had made it end in "ics" it resembled mathematics, I thought that the sublime and venerable art of mystification could no further go. If my fellow-pilgrim through this vale of woe, the average young man who arrives at Waterloo at 9.40 every morning with a cigarette in his mouth and a second-class season over his heart and vague aspirations in his soul, was half as mystified as I was, he has probably ere this decided that the science of success has all the disadvantages of algebra without any of the advantages of cricket, and that he may as well leave it alone lest evil should befall him. On the off-chance that he has come as yet to no decision about the science of success, I am determined to deal with the subject in a disturbingly candid manner. I feel that it is as dangerous to tell the truth about success as it is to tell the truth about the United States; but being thoroughly accustomed to the whistle of bullets round my head, I will nevertheless try.

Most writers on success are, through sheer goodness of heart, wickedly disingenuous. For the basis of their argument is that nearly any one who gives his mind to it can achieve success. This is, to put it briefly, untrue. The very central idea of success is separation from the multitude of plain men; it is perhaps the only idea common to all the various sorts of success—differentiation from the crowd. To address the population at large, and tell it how to separate itself from itself, is merely silly. I am now, of course, using the word success in its ordinary sense. If human nature were more perfect than it is, success in life would mean an intimate knowledge of one's self and the achievement of a philosophic inward calm, and such a goal might well be reached by the majority of mortals. But to us success signifies something else. It may be divided into four branches: (1) Distinction in pure or applied science. This is the least gross of all forms of success as we regard it, for it frequently implies poverty, and it does not by any means always imply fame. (2) Distinction in the arts. Fame and adulation are usually implied in this, though they do not commonly bring riches with them. (3) Direct influence and power over the material lives of other men; that is to say, distinction in politics, national or local. (4) Success in amassing money. This last is the commonest and easiest. Most forms of success will fall under one of these heads. Are they possible to that renowned and much-flattered person, the man in the street? They are not, and well you know it, all you professors of the science of success! Only a small minority of us can even become rich.

Happily, while it is true that success in its common acceptation is, by its very essence, impossible to the majority, there is an accompanying truth which adjusts the balance; to wit, that the majority do not desire success. This may seem a bold saying, but it is in accordance with the facts. Conceive the man in the street suddenly, by some miracle, invested with political power, and, of course, under the obligation to use it. He would be so upset, worried, wearied, and exasperated at the end of a week that he would be ready to give the eyes out of his head in order to get rid of it. As for success in science or in art, the average person's interest in such matters is so slight, compared with that of the man of science or the artist, that he cannot be said to have an interest in them. And supposing that distinction in them were thrust upon him he would rapidly lose that distinction by simple indifference and neglect. The average person certainly wants some money, and the average person does not usually rest until he has got as much as is needed for the satisfaction of his instinctive needs. He will move the heaven and earth of his environment to earn sufficient money for marriage in the "station" to which he has been accustomed; and precisely at that point his genuine desire for money will cease to be active. The average man has this in common with the most exceptional genius, that his career in its main contours is governed by his instincts. The average man flourishes and finds his ease in an atmosphere of peaceful routine. Men destined for success flourish and find their ease in an atmosphere of collision and disturbance. The two temperaments are diverse. Naturally the average man dreams vaguely, upon occasion; he dreams how nice it would be to be famous and rich. We all dream vaguely upon such things. But to dream vaguely is not to desire. I often tell myself that I would give anything to be the equal of Cinquevalli, the juggler, or to be the captain of the largest Atlantic liner. But the reflective part of me tells me that my yearning to emulate these astonishing personages is not a genuine desire, and that its realization would not increase my happiness.

To obtain a passably true notion of what happens to the mass of mankind in its progress from the cradle to the grave, one must not attempt to survey a whole nation, nor even a great metropolis, nor even a very big city like Manchester or Liverpool. These panoramas are so immense and confusing that they defeat the observing eye. It is better to take a small town of, say, twenty or thirty thousand inhabitants—such a town as most of us know, more or less intimately. The extremely few individuals whose instincts mark them out to take part in the struggle for success can be identified at once. For the first thing they do is to leave the town. The air of the town is not bracing enough for them. Their nostrils dilate for something keener. Those who are left form a microcosm which is representative enough of the world at large. Between the ages of thirty and forty they begin to sort themselves out. In their own sphere they take their places. A dozen or so politicians form the town council and rule the town. Half a dozen business men stand for the town's commercial activity and its wealth. A few others teach science and art, or are locally known as botanists, geologists, amateurs of music, or amateurs of some other art. These are the distinguished, and it will be perceived that they cannot be more numerous than they are. What of the rest? Have they struggled for success and been beaten? Not they. Do they, as they grow old, resemble disappointed men? Not they. They have fulfilled themselves modestly. They have got what they genuinely tried to get. They have never even gone near the outskirts of the battle for success. But they have not failed. The number of failures is surprisingly small. You see a shabby, disappointed, ageing man flit down the main street, and someone replies to your inquiry: "That's So-and-so, one of life's failures, poor fellow!" And the very tone in which the words are uttered proves the excessive rarity of the real failure. It goes without saying that the case of the handful who have left the town in search of the Success with the capital S has a tremendous interest of curiosity for the mass who remain. I will consider it.

THE SUCCESSFUL AND THE UNSUCCESSFUL

Having boldly stated that success is not, and cannot be, within grasp of the majority, I now proceed to state, as regards the minority, that they do not achieve it in the manner in which they are commonly supposed to achieve it. And I may add an expression of my thankfulness that they do not. The popular delusion is that success is attained by what I may call the "Benjamin Franklin" method. Franklin was a very great man; he united in his character a set of splendid qualities as various, in their different ways, as those possessed by Leonardo da Vinci. I have an immense admiration for him. But his Autobiography does make me angry. His Autobiography is understood to be a classic, and if you say a word against it in the United States you are apt to get killed. I do not, however, contemplate an immediate visit to the United States, and I shall venture to assert that Benjamin Franklin's Autobiography is a detestable book and a misleading book. I can recall only two other volumes which I would more willingly revile. One is *Samuel Budgett: The Successful Merchant*, and the other is *From Log Cabin to White House*, being the history of President Garfield. Such books may impose on boys, and it is conceivable that they do not harm boys (Franklin, by the way, began his Autobiography in the form of a letter to his son), but the grown man who can support them without nausea ought to go and see a doctor, for there is something wrong with him.

"I began now," blandly remarks Franklin, "to have some acquaintance among the young people of the town that were lovers of reading, with whom I spent my evenings very pleasantly; *and gained money by my industry and frugality.*" Or again: "It was about this time I conceived the bold and arduous project of arriving at moral perfection.... I made a little book, in which I allotted a page for each of the virtues. I ruled each page with red ink, so as to have seven columns, one for each day of the week.... I crossed these columns with thirteen red lines, marking the beginning of each line with the first letter of one of the virtues; on which line, and in its proper column, I might mark, by a little black spot, every fault I found upon examination to have been committed respecting that virtue, upon that day." Shade of Franklin, where'er thou art, this is really a little bit stiff! A man may be excused even such infamies of priggishness, but truly he ought not to go and write them down, especially to his son. And why the detail about red ink? If Franklin's son was not driven to evil courses by the perusal of that monstrous Autobiography, he must have been a man almost as astounding as his father. Now Franklin could only have written his "immortal classic" from one of three motives: (1) Sheer conceit. He was a prig, but he was not conceited. (2) A desire that others should profit by his mistakes. He never made any mistakes. Now and again he emphasizes some trifling error, but that is "only his fun." (3) A desire that others should profit by the recital of his virtuous sagacity to reach a similar success. The last was undoubtedly his principal motive. Honest fellow, who happened to be a genius! But the point is that his success was in no way the result of his virtuous sagacity. I would go further, and say that his dreadful virtuous sagacity often hindered his success.

No one is a worse guide to success than your typical successful man. He seldom understands the reasons of his own success; and when he is asked by a popular magazine to give his experiences for the benefit of the youth of a whole nation, it is impossible for him to be natural and sincere. He knows the kind of thing that is expected from him, and if he didn't come to London with half a crown in his pocket he probably did something equally silly, and he puts *that* down, and the note of the article or interview is struck, and good-bye to genuine truth! There recently appeared in a daily paper an autobiographic-didactic article by one of the world's richest men which was the most "inadequate" article of the sort that I have ever come across. Successful men forget so much of their lives! Moreover, nothing is easier than to explain an accomplished fact in a nice, agreeable, conventional way. The entire business of success is a gigantic tacit conspiracy on the part of the minority to deceive the majority.

Are successful men more industrious, frugal, and intelligent than men who are not successful? I maintain that they are not, and I have studied successful men at close quarters. One of the commonest characteristics of the successful man is his idleness, his immense capacity for wasting time. I stoutly assert that as a rule successful men are by habit comparatively idle. As for frugality, it is practically unknown among the successful classes: this statement applies with particular force to financiers. As for intelligence, I have over and over again been startled by the lack of intelligence in successful men. They are, indeed, capable of stupidities that would be the ruin of a plain clerk. And much of the talk in those circles which surround the successful man is devoted to the enumeration of instances of his lack of intelligence. Another point: successful men seldom succeed as the result of an ordered arrangement of their lives; they are the least methodical of creatures. Naturally when they have "arrived" they amuse themselves and impress the majority by being convinced that right from the start, with a steady eye on the goal, they had carefully planned every foot of the route.

No! Great success never depends on the practice of the humbler virtues, though it may occasionally depend on the practice of the prouder vices. Use industry, frugality, and common sense by all means, but do not expect that they will help you to success. Because they will not. I shall no doubt be told that what I have just written has an immoral tendency, and is a direct encouragement to sloth, thriftlessness, etc. One of our chief national faults is our hypocritical desire to suppress the truth on the pretext that to admit it would encourage sin, whereas the real explanation is that we are afraid of the truth. I will not be guilty of that fault. I do like to look a fact in the face without blinking. I am fully persuaded that, per head, there is more of the virtues in the unsuccessful majority than in the successful minority. In London alone are there not hundreds of miles of streets crammed with industry, frugality, and prudence? Some of the most brilliant men I have known have been failures, and not through lack of character either. And some of the least gifted have been marvellously successful. It is impossible to point to a single branch of human activity in which success can be explained by the conventional principles that find general acceptance. I hear you, O reader, murmuring to yourself: "This is all very well, but he is simply being paradoxical for his own diversion." I would that I could persuade you of my intense seriousness! I have endeavoured to show what does not make success. I will next endeavour to show what does make it. But my hope is forlorn.

THE INWARDNESS OF SUCCESS

Of course, one can no more explain success than one can explain Beethoven's C minor symphony. One may state what key it is written in, and make expert reflections upon its form, and catalogue its themes, and relate it to symphonies that preceded it and symphonies that followed it, but in the end one is reduced to saying that the C minor symphony is beautiful—because it is. In the same manner one is reduced to saying that the sole real difference between success and failure is that success succeeds. This being frankly admitted at the outset, I will allow myself to assert that there are three sorts of success. Success A is the accidental sort. It is due to the thing we call chance, and to nothing else. We are all of us still very superstitious, and the caprices of chance have a singular effect upon us. Suppose that I go to Monte Carlo and announce to a friend my firm conviction that red will turn up next time, and I back red for the maximum and red does turn up; my friend, in spite of his intellect, will vaguely attribute to me a mysterious power. Yet chance alone would be responsible. If I did that six times running all the players at the table would be interested in me. If I did it a dozen times all the players in the Casino would regard me with awe. Yet chance alone would be responsible. If I did it eighteen times my name would be in every newspaper in Europe. Yet chance alone would be responsible. I should be, in that department of human activity, an extremely successful man, and the vast majority of people would instinctively credit me with gifts that I do not possess.

If such phenomena of superstition can occur in an affair where the agency of chance is open and avowed, how much more probable is it that people should refuse to be satisfied with the explanation of "sheer accident" in affairs where it is to the interest of the principal actors to conceal the rôle played by chance! Nevertheless, there can be no doubt in the minds of persons who have viewed success at close quarters that a proportion of it is due solely and utterly to chance. Successful men flourish to-day, and have flourished in the past, who have no quality whatever to differentiate them from the multitude. Red has turned up for them a sufficient number of times, and the universal superstitious instinct not to believe in chance has accordingly surrounded them with a halo. It is merely ridiculous to say, as some do say, that success is never due to chance alone. Because nearly everybody is personally acquainted with reasonable proof, on a great or a small scale, to the contrary.

The second sort of success, B, is that made by men who, while not gifted with first-class talents, have, beyond doubt, the talent to succeed. I should describe these men by saying that, though they deserve something, they do not deserve the dazzling reward known as success. They strike us as overpaid. We meet them in all professions and trades, and we do not really respect them. They excite our curiosity, and perhaps our envy. They may rise very high indeed, but they must always be unpleasantly conscious of a serious reservation in our attitude towards them. And if they could read their obituary notices they would assuredly discern therein a certain chilliness, however kindly we acted up to our great national motto of *De mortuis nil nisi bunkum*. It is this class of success which puzzles the social student. How comes it that men without any other talent possess a mysterious and indefinable talent to succeed?

Well, it seems to me that such men always display certain characteristics. And the chief of these characteristics is the continual, insatiable *wish* to succeed. They are preoccupied with the idea of succeeding. We others are not so preoccupied. We dream of success at intervals, but we have not the passion for success. We don't lie awake at nights pondering upon it.

The second characteristic of these men springs naturally from the first. They are always on the look-out. This does not mean that they are industrious. I stated in a previous article my belief that as a rule successful men are not particularly industrious. A man on a raft with his shirt for a signal cannot be termed industrious, but he will keep his eyes open for a sail on the horizon. If he simply lies down and goes to sleep he may miss the chance of his life, in a very special sense. The man with the talent to succeed is the man on the raft who never goes to sleep. His indefatigable orb sweeps the main from sunset to sunset. Having sighted a sail, he gets up on his hind legs and waves that shirt in so determined a manner that the ship is bound to see him and take him off. Occasionally he plunges into the sea, risking sharks and other perils. If he doesn't "get there," we hear nothing of him. If he does, some person will ultimately multiply by ten the number of sharks that he braved: that person is called a biographer.

Let me drop the metaphor. Another characteristic of these men is that they seem to have the exact contrary of what is known as common sense. They will become enamoured of some enterprise which infallibly impresses the average common-sense person as a mad and hopeless enterprise. The average common-sense person will demolish the hopes of that enterprise by incontrovertible argument. He will point out that it is foolish on the face of it, that it has never been attempted before, and that it responds to no need of humanity. He will say to himself: "This fellow with his precious enterprise has a twist in his brain. He can't reply to my arguments, and yet he obstinately persists in going on." And the man destined to success does go on. Perhaps the enterprise fails; it often fails; and then the average common-sense person expends much breath in "I told you so's." But the man continues to be on the look-out. His thirst is unassuaged; his taste for enterprises foredoomed to failure is incurable. And one day some enterprise foredoomed to failure develops into a success. We all hear of it. We all open our mouths and gape. Of the failures we have heard nothing. Once the man has achieved success, the thing becomes a habit with him. The difference between a success and a failure is often so slight that a reputation for succeeding will ensure success, and a reputation for failing will ensure failure. Chance plays an important part in such careers, but not a paramount part. One can only say that it is more useful to have luck at the beginning than later on. These "men of success" generally have pliable temperaments. They are not frequently un-moral, but they regard a conscience as a good servant and a bad master. They live in an atmosphere of compromise.

There remains class C of success—the class of sheer high merit. I am not a pessimist, nor am I an optimist. I try to arrive at the truth, and I should say that in putting success C at ten per cent. of the sum total of all successes, I am being generous to class C. Not that I believe that vast quantities of merit go unappreciated. My reason for giving to Class C only a modest share is the fact that there is so little sheer high merit. And does it not stand to reason that high merit must be very exceptional? This sort of success needs no explanation, no accounting for. It is the justification of our singular belief in the principle of the triumph of justice, and it is among natural phenomena perhaps the only justification that can be advanced for that belief. And certainly when we behold the spectacle of genuine distinguished merit gaining, without undue delay and without the sacrifice of dignity or of conscience, the applause of the kind-hearted but obtuse and insensible majority of the human race, we have fair reason to hug ourselves.

VIII

THE PETTY ARTIFICIALITIES

The phrase "petty artificialities," employed by one of the correspondents in the great Simple Life argument, has stuck in my mind, although I gave it a plain intimation that it was no longer wanted there. Perhaps it sheds more light than I had at first imagined on the mental state of the persons who use it when they wish to arraign the conditions of "modern life." A vituperative epithet is capable of making a big show. "Artificialities" is a sufficiently scornful word, but when you add "petty" you somehow give the quietus to the pretensions of modern life. Modern life had better hide its diminished head, after that. Modern life is settled and done for—in the opinion of those who have thrown the dart. Only it isn't done for, really, you know. "Petty," after all, means nothing in that connexion. Are there, then, artificialities which are not "petty," which are noble, large, and grand? "Petty" means merely that the users of the word are just a little cross and out of temper. What they think they object to is artificialities of any kind, and so to get rid of their spleen they refer to "petty" artificialities. The device is a common one, and as brilliant as it is futile. Rude adjectives are like blank cartridge. They impress a vain people, including the birds of the air, but they do no execution.

At the same time, let me admit that I deeply sympathize with the irritated users of the impolite phrase "petty artificialities." For it does at any rate show a "divine discontent"; it does prove a high dissatisfaction with conditions which at best are not the final expression of the eternal purpose. It does make for a sort of crude and churlish righteousness. I well know that feeling which induces one to spit out savagely the phrase "petty artificialities of modern life." One has it usually either on getting up or on going to bed. What a petty artificial business it is, getting up, even for a male! Shaving! Why shave? And then going to a drawer and choosing a necktie. Fancy an immortal soul, fancy a fragment of the eternal and indestructible energy, which exists from everlasting to everlasting, deliberately expending its activity on the choice of a necktie! Why a necktie? Then one goes downstairs and exchanges banal phrases with other immortals. And one can't start breakfast immediately, because some sleepy mortal is late.

Why babble? Why wait? Why not say straight out: "Go to the deuce, all of you! Here it's nearly ten o'clock, and me anxious to begin living the higher life at once instead of fiddling around in petty artificialities. Shut up, every one of you. Give me my bacon instantly, and let me gobble it down quick and be off. I'm sick of your ceremonies!" This would at any rate not be artificial. It would save time. And if a similar policy were strictly applied through the day, one could retire to a well-earned repose in the full assurance that the day had been simplified. The time for living the higher life, the time for pushing forward those vast schemes of self-improvement which we all cherish, would decidedly have been increased. One would not have that maddening feeling, which one so frequently does have when the shades of night are falling fast, that the day had been "frittered away." And yet—and yet—I gravely doubt whether this wholesale massacre of those poor petty artificialities would bring us appreciably nearer the millennium.

For there is one thing, and a thing of fundamental importance, which the revolutionists against petty artificialities always fail to appreciate, and that is the necessity and the value of convention. I cannot in a paragraph deal effectively with this most difficult and complex question. I can only point the reader to analogous phenomena in the arts. All the arts are a conventionalization, an ordering of nature. Even in a garden you put the plants in rows, and you subordinate the well-being of one to the general well-being. The sole difference between a garden and the wild woods is a petty artificiality. In writing a sonnet you actually cramp the profoundest emotional conceptions into a length and a number of lines and a jingling of like sounds arbitrarily fixed beforehand! Wordsworth's "The world is too much with us" is a solid, horrid mass of petty artificiality. Why couldn't the fellow say what he meant and have done with it, instead of making "powers" rhyme with "ours," and worrying himself to use exactly a hundred and forty syllables? As for music, the amount of time that must have been devoted to petty artificiality in the construction of an affair like Bach's Chaconne is simply staggering. Then look at pictures, absurdly confined in frames, with their ingenious contrasts of light and shade and mass against mass. Nothing but petty artificiality! In other words, nothing but "form"— "form" which is the basis of all beauty, whether material or otherwise.

Now, what form is in art, conventions (petty artificialities) are in life. Just as you can have too much form in art, so you can have too much convention in life. But no art that is not planned in form is worth consideration, and no life that is not planned in convention can ever be satisfactory. Convention is not the essence of life, but it is the protecting garment and preservative of life, and it is also one very valuable means by which life can express itself. It is largely symbolic; and symbols, while being expressive, are also great time-savers. The despisers of petty artificialities should think of this. Take the striking instance of that pettiest artificiality, leaving cards. Well, searchers after the real, what would you substitute for it? If you dropped it and substituted nothing, the result would tend towards a loosening of the bonds of society, and it would tend towards the diminution of the number of your friends. And if you dropped it and tried to substitute something less artificial and more real, you would accomplish no more than you accomplish with cards, you would inconvenience everybody, and waste a good deal of your own time. I cannot too strongly insist that the basis of convention is a symbolism, primarily meant to display a regard for the feelings of other people. If you do not display a regard for the feelings of other people, you may as well go and live on herbs in the desert. And if you are to display such a regard you cannot do it more expeditiously, at a smaller outlay of time and brains, than by adopting the code of convention now generally practised. It comes to this—that you cannot have all the advantages of living in the desert while you are living in a society. It would be delightful for you if you could, but you can't.

There are two further reasons for the continuance of conventionality. And one is the mysterious but indisputable fact that the full beauty of an activity is never brought out until it is subjected to discipline and strict ordering and nice balancing. A life without petty artificiality would be the life of a tiger in the forest. A beautiful life, perhaps, a life of "burning bright," but not reaching the highest ideal of beauty! Laws and rules, forms and ceremonies are good in themselves, from a merely æsthetic point of view, apart from their social value and necessity.

And the other reason is that one cannot always be at the full strain of "self-improvement," and "evolutionary progress," and generally beating the big drum. Human nature will not stand it. There is, if we will only be patient, ample time for the "artificial" as well as for the "real." Those persons who think that there isn't, ought to return to school and learn arithmetic. Supposing that all "petty artificialities" were suddenly swept away, and we were able to show our regard and consideration for our fellow creatures by the swift processes of thought alone, we should find ourselves with a terrible lot of time hanging heavy on our hands. We can no more spend all our waking hours in consciously striving towards higher things than we can dine exclusively off jam. What frightful prigs we should become if we had nothing to do but cultivate our noblest faculties! I beg the despisers of artificiality to reflect upon these observations, however incomplete these observations may be, and to consider whether they would be quite content if they got what they are crying out for.

IX

THE SECRET OF CONTENT

I have said lightly à propos of the conclusion arrived at by several correspondents and by myself that the cry for the simple life was merely a new form of the old cry for happiness, that I would explain what it was that made life worth living for me. The word has gone forth, and I must endeavour to redeem my promise. But I do so with qualms and with diffidence. First, there is the natural instinct against speaking of that which is in the core of one's mind. Second, there is the fear, nearly amounting to certainty, of being misunderstood or not comprehended at all. And third, there is the absurd insufficiency of space. However!... For me, spiritual content (I will not use the word "happiness," which implies too much) springs essentially from no mental or physical facts. It springs from the spiritual fact that there is something higher in man than the mind, and that that something can control the mind. Call that something the soul, or what you will. My sense of security amid the collisions of existence lies in the firm consciousness that just as my body is the servant of my mind, so is my mind the servant of *me*. An unruly servant, but a servant—and possibly getting less unruly every day! Often have I said to that restive brain: "Now, O mind, sole means of communication between the divine *me* and all external phenomena, you are not a free agent; you are a subordinate; you are nothing but a piece of machinery; and obey me you *shall*."

The mind can only be conquered by regular meditation, by deciding beforehand what direction its activity ought to take, and insisting that its activity takes that direction; also by never leaving it idle, undirected, masterless, to play at random like a child in the streets after dark. This is extremely difficult, but it can be done, and it is marvellously well worth doing. The fault of the epoch is the absence of meditativeness. A sagacious man will strive to correct in himself the faults of his epoch. In some deep ways the twelfth century had advantages over the twentieth. It practised meditation. The twentieth does Sandow exercises. Meditation (I speak only for myself) is the least dispensable of the day's doings. What do I force my mind to meditate upon? Upon various things, but chiefly upon one.

Namely, that Force, Energy, Life—the Incomprehensible has many names—is indestructible, and that, in the last analysis, there is only one single, unique Force, Energy, Life. Science is gradually reducing all elements to one element. Science is making it increasingly difficult to conceive matter apart from spirit. Everything lives. Even my razor gets "tired." And the fatigue of my razor is no more nor less explicable than my fatigue after a passage of arms with my mind. The Force in it, and in me, has been transformed, not lost. All Force is the same force. Science just now has a tendency to call it electricity; but I am indifferent to such baptisms. The same Force pervades my razor, my cow in my field, and the central *me* which dominates my mind: the same force in different stages of evolution. And that Force persists forever. In such paths do I compel my mind to walk daily. Daily it has to recognize that the mysterious Ego controlling it is a part of that divine Force which exists from everlasting to everlasting, and which, in its ultimate atoms, nothing can harm. By such a course of training, even the mind, the coarse, practical mind, at last perceives that worldly accidents don't count.

"But," you will exclaim, "this is nothing but the immortality of the soul over again!" Well, in a slightly more abstract form, it is. (I never said I had discovered anything new.) I do not permit myself to be dogmatic about the persistence of personality, or even of individuality after death. But, in basing my physical and mental life on the assumption that there is something in me which is indestructible and essentially changeless, I go no further than science points. Yes, if it gives you pleasure, let us call it the immortality of the soul. If I miss my train, or my tailor disgraces himself, or I lose that earthly manifestation of Force that happens to be dearest to me, I say to my mind: "Mind, concentrate your powers upon the full realization of the fact that I, your master, am immortal and beyond the reach of accidents." And my mind, knowing by this time that I am a hard master, obediently does so. Am I, a portion of the Infinite Force that existed billions of years ago, and which will exist billions of years hence, going to allow myself to be worried by any terrestrial physical or mental event? I am not. As for the vicissitudes of my body, that servant of my servant, it had better keep its place, and not make too much fuss. Not that any fuss occurring in either of these outward envelopes of the eternal *me* could really disturb me. The eternal is calm; it has the best reason for being so.

So you say to yourselves: "Here is a man in a penny weekly paper advocating daily meditation upon the immortality of the soul as a cure for discontent and unhappiness! A strange phenomenon!" That it should be strange is an indictment of the epoch. My only reply to you is this: Try it. Of course, I freely grant that such meditation, while it "casts out fear," slowly kills desire and makes for a certain high indifference; and that the extinguishing of desire, with an accompanying indifference, be it high or low, is bad for youth. But I am not a youth, and to-day I am writing for those who have tasted disillusion: which youth has not. Yet I would not have you believe that I scorn the brief joys of this world. My attitude towards them would fain be that of Socrates, as stated by the incomparable Marcus Aurelius: "He knew how to lack, and how to enjoy, those things in the lack whereof most men show themselves weak; and in the fruition, intemperate."

Besides commanding my mind to dwell upon the indestructibly and final omnipotence of the Force which is me, I command it to dwell upon the logical consequence of that *unity* of force which science is now beginning to teach. The same essential force that is *me* is also *you*. Says the Indian proverb: "I met a hundred men on the road to Delhi, and they were all my brothers." Yes, and they were all my twin brothers, if I may so express it, and a thousand times closer to me even than the common conception of twin brothers. We are all of us the same in essence; what separates us is merely differences in our respective stages of evolution. Constant reflection upon this fact must produce that universal sympathy which alone can produce a positive content. It must do away with such ridiculous feelings as blame, irritation, anger, resentment. It must establish in the mind an all-embracing tolerance. Until a man can look upon the drunkard in his drunkenness, and upon the wife-beater in his brutality, with pure and calm compassion; until his heart goes out instinctively to every other manifestation of the unique Force; until he is surcharged with an eager and unconquerable benevolence towards everything that lives; until he has utterly abandoned the presumptuous practice of judging and condemning—he will never attain real content. "Ah!" you exclaim again, "he has nothing newer to tell us than that 'the greatest of these is charity'!" I have not. It may strike you as excessively funny, but I have discovered nothing newer than that. I merely remind you of it. Thus it is, twins on the road to Delhi, by continual meditation upon the indestructibility of Force, that I try to cultivate calm, and by continual meditation upon the oneness of Force that I try to cultivate charity, being fully convinced that in calmness and in charity lies the secret of a placid if not ecstatic happiness. It is often said that no thinking person can be happy in this world. My view is that the more a man thinks the more happy he is likely to be. I have spoken. I am overwhelmingly aware that I have spoken crudely, abruptly, inadequately, confusedly.

THE END

Printed in the United Kingdom by
Lightning Source UK Ltd., Milton Keynes
139315UK00001B/1/P

9 781406 866735